T0292544

In English and Transliterated Malayalam and Syriac

My FIRST Holy Qurbono Words for Children

From the Orthodox Divine Liturgy
of the
Aramaic Syriac Tradition

GITA GEORGE-HATCHER

WestBow Press books may be ordered through booksellers or by contacting:

WestBow Press
A Division of Thomas Nelson & Zondervan
1663 Liberty Drive
Bloomington, IN 47403
www.westbowpress.com
1 (866) 928-1240

ISBN: 978-1-9736-9229-4 (sc)
ISBN: 978-1-9736-9230-0 (e)

Library of Congress Control Number: 2020909927

Print information available on the last page.

WestBow Press rev. date: 07/28/2020

WESTBOW
PRESS®
A DIVISION OF THOMAS NELSON
& ZONDERVAN

My FIRST Holy Qurbono Words for Children

Temple/Devalayam/Haykla

On Sunday, we go to the Temple to worship God.
"Qurbono" or "Qurbana" means
"Offering" in Jesus' language.

Church/Palli/Ito

Is made up of the people of God worshipping together.

Jesus Christ/ Yeshu Meshiha/ Yeshu M'Shiho

We worship the Holy Trinity – One God - the Father, His Son Jesus Christ and the Holy Spirit. Jesus died on the cross for our sins and rose again on the third day so we may all be saved!

At the Temple we are quiet and respectful
as we pray and worship.

Table/Bema

The Bema has a cross on it and is in front of the altar.

The priest, deacons and altar servers stand at the Bema while we all sing the morning prayers.

Psalms
Sangeerthanam
Mazmooro

We sing from the Psalms of King David, and read from the other Books of the Old Testament before the Holy Qurbono begins.

Curtain/ Thirusheela/ Satro/Weelo

The curtain covers the altar and has a beautiful cross on it.

Altar/Madhbaha/ Madhbaho

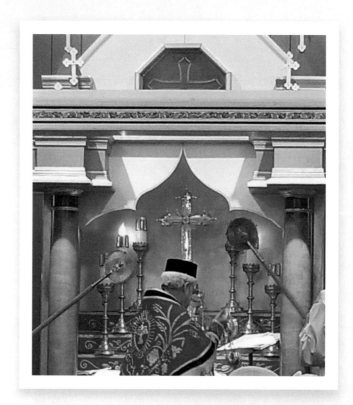

The curtain opens when the Holy Qurbono begins.
We sing, we chant, we stand and pay attention.

Cross/ Kurishu/Sleebo

The cross on the altar helps us to remember
the sacrifice of our Lord Jesus Christ.

Icons/Holy Pictures

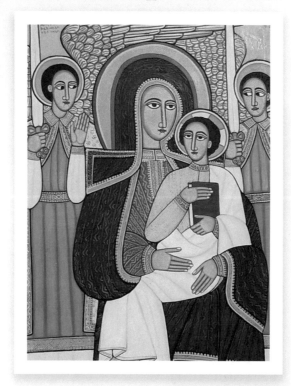

Icons teach us about God, the Bible, and
the lives of holy people. Icons remind us
that all the saints are praying with us.

Priest or Father/Achen/Kohno

Father leads us in worship and offers the Holy
Qurbono for us. He represents our Lord Jesus Christ
at the altar and wears beautiful vestments.

The Deacon and the Reader help the Priest at the Altar

Deacon

Shemashen

M'Shamshono

Reader/Koroyo

Angel Fans
Marbasa
Marbohthe

The sound of the fans with the bells tells
us that the angels are with us.

Gospel /Evangelion

Father reads from the Gospel.

Gospel means "Good News."
There are four Gospels in the
Bible – they are the Gospels
of St. Matthew, St. Mark,
St. Luke, and St. John.

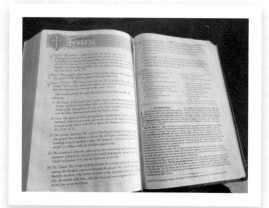

Censer/Dhoopakutti
Phirmo

The incense shows us that God is with us and
hears our prayers as they rise to heaven.

Father blesses the censer in the name of
the Holy Trinity so he can bless us!

Peace/Samadhaanam/Shlomo

The peace is given from the altar...

...and is passed on until each person in
the Church receives the peace.

Prayer/Praarthana/Slootho

Father prays for all who have asked him to
remember them during the Holy Qurbono
while we sing, "This is the time of prayer."

Chalice/Kaasa/Koso
Paten/Pilaasa/Fiyalo

Offerings of bread and wine are placed
in the paten and chalice.

Holy Communion/Holy Mysteries

The Holy Spirit changes the bread and wine into the Holy Mysteries that Father gives to us so we can have eternal life with our Lord Jesus Christ.

Holy Trinity – One God, Father, Son and Holy Spirit

Father blesses us many times in the name of the Holy Trinity and at the end, asks us to pray for him always.

Blessed Bread (Brukhso)

After the liturgy is over, Father blesses us and gives us blessed bread called brukhso.